SYLLABUS OF ERRORS

Princeton Series of Contemporary Poets

Susan Stewart, *series editor*

For other titles in the Princeton Series of Contemporary Poets see page 99

SYLLABUS OF ERRORS

Poems

Troy Jollimore

PRINCETON UNIVERSITY PRESS
Princeton & Oxford

The author would like to express his deep gratitude to the John Simon Guggenheim Foundation for their support in the writing of this book.

Copyright © 2016 by Princeton University Press
Published by Princeton University Press, 41 William Street,
 Princeton, New Jersey 08540
In the United Kingdom: Princeton University Press, 6 Oxford Street,
 Woodstock, Oxfordshire OX20 1TW

press.princeton.edu
Jacket photograph: *Backyard baseball, about one year old. April 15, 2005,*
 copyright © 2005 by Byron Wolfe.

ISBN 978–0–691–16758–9

ISBN (pbk.) 978-0-691-16768-8

Library of Congress Control Number: 2014959228

British Library Cataloging-in-Publication Data is available

This book has been composed in Adobe Garamond

Printed on acid-free paper. ∞

Printed in the United States of America

10 9 8 7 6 5 4 3 2 1

for Heather

Sir, we are a nest of singing birds.

—SAMUEL JOHNSON

Contents

I ON BIRDSONG

On Birdsong 3
Inventory 4
Ache and Echo 5
On the Origins of Things 11
Critique of Judgment 12
Homer 13
Oriole 15
Past Imperfect 16

II ON BEAUTY

On Beauty 23
Syllabus of Errors 24
Cutting Room 26
My Book 29
Going Viral 30
Bone 32
Possession 35
Death by Landscape 36
Second Wind 37
The Black-Capped Chickadees of Martha's Vineyard 38

III ON BLINDNESS

On Blindness 43
The Apples 45
Charlie Brown 47

Some Men   49
The Proselytizers   51
Universal   52
Photograph   54
Polaroid Model 1000 OneStep, Circa 1978   55
Ars Poetica   57
The New Joys   59

IV WHEN YOU LIFT THE AVOCADO TO YOUR MOUTH

Tamara   63
The Task   64
More Broken than Yours   66
Fireworks   68
Lament   69
The Fourteen-Hour Orgasm   71
Not Enough   72
Poem for the Abandoned Titan Missile Silos Just North of
    Chico, California   76
Autumn Day (after Rilke)   77
The Small Rain   78
When You Lift the Avocado to Your Mouth   79

V VERTIGO

Vertigo   83

VI CONCLUDING UNSCIENTIFIC POSTSCRIPT

[maybe I just need time to grieve]   95

NOTES AND ACKNOWLEDGMENTS   97

I ON BIRDSONG

If my readers wish to understand bird-music, they must assume that birds are not automatic musical boxes, but sound-lovers, who cultivate the pursuit of sound-combinations as an art, as truly as we have cultivated our arts of a similarly aesthetic character. This art becomes to many of them a real object of life, no less real than the pursuit of food or the maintenance of a family.

—WALTER GARSTANG, *SONGS OF THE BIRDS* (1922)

ON BIRDSONG

Poison, in proportion, is medicinal.
Medicine, ill-meted, can be terminal.

Brute noise, deftly repeated, becomes musical.
An exit viewed from elsewhere is an entrance.

The conjuror entrances a vast audience.
The hymn that's resurrected from the hymnal

aspires, as we wish to, to the spiritual,
but is slow to disentangle from the sensual.

The evening light, refracted, terminates the day.
(A faction is a fraction of an integral.)

What would we say to the cardinal or jay,
given wings that could mimic their velocities?

How many wintery ferocities
are encompassed in their shrill inhuman canticles?

INVENTORY

Take inventory. Invent a story
about the people you have hurt.
Begin with yourself. The harm I've done
comes on this journey with me. He walks
ahead on the trail, or follows a dozen
paces behind. At night we stop
together. I try not to feel ashamed
of him, his decaying robes, his loathsome,
unwashed feet, so much like mine.
We don't talk much. But two nights ago,
the campfire dying between us, I found
I could no longer stifle my rage, I wanted
to be rid of him so badly, and so
I mustered my anger and said, *You only*
get seven pairs of shoes to carry you
through this life, and you've already used up
four. Silence. The call of a whippoorwill
in the fields. At last he looked up.
That might be. But know that I'm willing to go
barefoot at the end, if that's what it takes.

ACHE AND ECHO

1

Anything can be beautiful: a discarded
Taco Bell wrapper, an industrial park,
a strip mall, a bloodstain, a bruise, a corpse:

you just need to see it from the right angle,
in the right light, and in a spirit
of equanimity, open-mindedness,

and receptivity. Isn't this
what twentieth-century artists were trying
to tell us? No, they were trying to tell us

that anything could be art. As for beauty,
they held it in contempt, they thought beauty
made us bad people, blind to the plight

of the poor, to the possibility of change.
That wasn't their nuttiest notion, either.
Not by a longshot. But me, I can't

give up my beauty, I'm an addict, a beauty
fiend; if you want to take it away
you're going to have to pry it from my cold dead hands.

2

Give back the ache that echoed in
my heart. Return to me the ache
and the echo of the ache I felt

in Orchid Park. Send back to me
the loose-strung ache that echoed in
the ark that is my heart. Retrace

the arc a happy heart might make.
Sing back to me the song we sang
in the outer dark, the art we make

of the ache we felt when we traced the arc
of the last falling star to fall.
And stir me, stir me with the spoon

you used to hide the moon. Then stir
the echo of my ache. My melody
has fallen out of tune.

3

One: what pleases, what disgusts,
is only skin deep. Like the beast who becomes
a handsome man at the end of the film.

Two: 'tis thinking makes it so.
What troubles is in the beholder's eye.
Or should that be the beholden?

Three: it was born from the womb of death,
or so it is said. You have met its brothers
skulking in the bushes with their video recorders.

Four: it is what truth is, where that
is all we know, and all we need
to know. Pretty is as privilege does.

Like a man who will happily murder a thousand
songbirds, if need be,
just to nab one perfect specimen.

4

At which point it is obligatory
to make mention of Pope Urban VIII,
who had the songbirds in the Vatican

gardens slaughtered, to create
a quiet sanctuary in which a
great and moral man

might suitably reflect
on such topics
as beauty, mercy, and grace.

5

Does every man, handsome or no,
contain a hidden beast? Is that
why pretty girls won't meet my eye?

Whoever it was thought to install
that scatter of houses, that precise
and poignant human outpost, in

that hilly spot beneath the dark
erasure we call sky, should really
be commended: such a perfect

counterpoint, such a revealing
object lesson in the plight
of mortal aspirations in

the face of the indifferent. Not
the pain of being, but the pain
of being some particular body,

of dragging a narrative behind you,
like a swimmer tangled up
in heavy nets, feeling the ocean,

its whole weight, beneath him. Similar
to sitting on a bench named for
some fallen hero or forgotten

poet and wishing one of those flare-winged
dashes of unabashed color, whose names
you have tried to learn but can never quite

remember, would pause and plummet
in mid-bombardment and alight
on your outstretched, expectant hand,

on your shoulder, on your tongue. *Stay
awhile,* as Faust said to his life,
you are so beautiful.

ON THE ORIGINS OF THINGS

Everyone knows that the moon started out
as a renegade fragment of the sun, a solar
flare that fled that hellish furnace
and congealed into a flat frozen pond suspended
between the planets. But did you know
that anger began as music, played
too often and too loudly by drunken musicians
at weddings and garden parties? Or that turtles
evolved from knuckles, ice from tears, and darkness
from misunderstanding? As for the dominant
thesis regarding the origin of love, I
abstain from comment, nor will I allow
myself to address the idea that dance
began as a kiss, that happiness was
an accidental import from Spain, that the ancient
game of jump-the-fire gave rise
to politics. But I will confess
that I began as an astronomer—a liking
for bright flashes, vast distances, unreachable
things, a hand stretched always toward
the furthest limit—and that my longing
for you has never taken me far
from that original desire, to inscribe
a comet's orbit around the walls
of our city, to gently stroke the surface of the stars.

CRITIQUE OF JUDGMENT

> . . . lyrebirds in the adjacent New England National Park were found
> to have flutelike elements in their song, a sound not heard in other
> populations of superb lyrebirds. Further analysis of the song showed
> that the phrase contained elements of two popular tunes of the 1930s,
> "Mosquito Dance" and "The Keel Row."
> —DAVID ROTHENBERG, *WHY BIRDS SING*

Reason informs us that birdsong is sublime
but can't be beautiful: beauty is conferred
solely by operations of the human mind.
Meanwhile, from that low-hanging branch, the lyrebird

is waging an ongoing, spirited battle
against philosophy. Its melodious rebuttals
owe a little something, I've just realized,
to "That'll Be the Day," as immortalized

by Buddy Holly and the Crickets. Tell me, is
a song a living thing? Does a song possess a shelf life?
A half-life? Will your favorite song enjoy an afterlife?
Do you have songbirds in your pockets? Is

there time for one last harvest? Would you like to file
an objection once the lyrebird is done with his?

HOMER

Schliemann is outside, digging. He's not
not calling a spade a spade.
The stadium where the Greeks once played
used to stand on this very spot.

Each night, Penelope, operating
in mythical time, unspools the light
gray orb Schliemann has just unearthed. Come daylight,
her hands will re-stitch it. The suitors sigh, waiting.

And each night I'd watch as my hero curled
himself round home plate, as if he were going
to bat for me. And I'd hold my breath, knowing
a strong enough shot might be heard round the world.

One must imagine Penelope.
One must imagine Penelope happy.
One must imagine Schliemann excavating
the dugouts and outfields of Troy, carbon-dating

the box score stats and the ticket stubs
he pulls from the lurid dirt. He rubs
the remains of Achilles' rage on his white shirt.
What does not kill you can still hurt.

Penelope's suitors are striking out,
one after another. Their sad swings and misses.
They can't even get to first base. She'll cut
the stitches once more, then blow them all kisses.

Odysseus won't care that the orb is undone.
He'll take a swing at it with all his might.
The ball takes flight. Odysseus takes flight.
It feels to Penelope like he's been gone

since the dawn of mankind, but he's already zoomed
round third and flies like an arrow toward home,
as the unearthly orb trails its guts in the air—
the yarn fanning out like Penelope's hair—

not knowing yet whether to fall foul or fair.

ORIOLE

A bend in the river.
A flaw in the surface.
How many continents
has this lone oriole
crossed to come balance
on our sagging clothesline,
and what urgent thing
is he trying to tell us?
That those who could translate
his song are lagging
a thousand miles
behind? Or that those
who can speak both his tongue
and ours have not yet
been born, that we will go
into the ground
and a thousand years pass
before their eyes open,
the wayward atoms
of our nests and tongues
having been dispersed,
reassigned, and repurposed
into their bright,
unforeseeable bodies?

PAST IMPERFECT

Because my image
of it is flickering,
wavering like a bad connection,

I can tell I'm not
the only one dreaming
of the Halifax Public Gardens tonight.

There must be a thousand
brains, at least,
plugged into this portal, sharing this channel,

this wavelength,
judging by the way
the edges slant off into soft static fuzz,

as if the whole picture
were under attack
by swarms of gray midges, or viewed through a lens

of murky lake water,
and even the stuff
in the center, on which I train my attention—

the ducks, like overstuffed
businessmen after a meal,
the pond with its crisp skim of scum

that has gathered in sheltered
pockets tucked close to
the shore—these too warp and bend, as if

I were viewing a movie
shot with equipment
salvaged from somewhere in Eastern Europe

after some war or
collapse, or filmed
by a perpetually distracted and, to judge

by the general coloration
of what I can see,
terminally disenchanted cinema-

tographer. Still, if I
focus, I can just
barely make out the shack where they sell

the ice cream and chips,
hastily sketched
like a hermit's hut in a Japanese painting,

and as the scroll
unfurls, if I turn my head,
that part of me that moves freely

through time detaches
itself from the part
of me that is pinned to the present, fetches

the bag that he packed
last night, and sets off
walking, casually, through the gardens

on his way to somewhere
even more distant:
the kitchen of my childhood, perhaps,

where my mother scrapes
the inside of a white plastic
bowl with a red-and-white plastic utensil

and stares out the window
as if she is trying
to imagine the set of white rooms in which

I now live. Or is he
going even further
back, to see her before I existed,

when she was a child,
not yet rendered mortal
by the sickness I would one day once

have been? Try
as I might, I can't say
for sure. I only know that he goes

and I stay, and that
the distance between
his going and my staying is the distance

between two adjacent
piano keys, two
consecutive letters of the alphabet,

the distance between
a word and its
translation into a now defunct language,

this distance that wants
nothing more than to stand
in the way of my loving this world, this world

that, though it wants nothing
more than to fling back
against me the sad siege engines of my

incessant attempts
at love,
I love.

II ON BEAUTY

the Airs which belong to Birds have
led our lives to be these things instead of Kings

—CHARLES OLSON

ON BEAUTY

Beauty, some have ventured, is proportional:
the right relative ratio of the actual

against the actual. Others hypothesize
that beauty's roots lie buried in the sexual,

insisting that aesthetics are relational:
the eye of the beholder is the noumenal

perceiving core, where spores of the phenomenal
sprout into lit-screen images. The visual

is permeated, down to the foundational,
with lust, with longing. Say it: we are animals,

which does not mean that we must all be criminals,
but only that desire is constitutional,

that we are fixed to perpetrate the species—
I meant *perpetuate*—as if our duty

were coupled with our terror. As if beauty
itself were but a syllabus of errors.

SYLLABUS OF ERRORS

You will first treat of the restricted light,
then, having achieved full adequacy
in this, of the free light, and finally, after
many exercises and much
disciplined contemplation, you will treat
of the light of luminous bodies.
Only then will you be ready
to make a study of love, of the void
that precipitates longing, of the soft tissues
that compose the kissing organs in humans,
the slow, cold fire these organs encompass.
Young women, their hearts. Passion, the diverse
expressions of and the obstructions thereto.
Whence comes the construction of children, then children,
the neglect and abandonment of. Having mastered
this, you will next turn to the pursuit
of competence in the fields of cartography,
of argumentation, of the imitation of beasts,
and of archery. As it comes to the arrow
in midair that the bow is the only
home it will ever really know,
and that it does not love the target at all,
so the seeds of delayed understanding
will come to you, drifting softly from some
high branch or low cloud to lodge in your hair,
on a Tuesday morning, perhaps. Whence come tears.
Whence comes the tuning of faint melodies
voiced by devices of ancient assembly.
Whence the correction of orbits, the rotation
of the eyes or of songbirds when the one

draws the other after. Why a prick
to the syrinx may still the heart of a man.
Whence frenzy by virtue of illness. Whence envy.
Whence shame. Whence trembling. Whence sleep. A figure
to show whence comes the semen. Whence urine.
Whence milk. Thunderbolts, their fatal capacity.
Joy, the diverse simulacra of.
Of the habits of men. Of ceaseless sobbing.

CUTTING ROOM

> Sooner or later everyone needs a haircut.
> —*THE MAN WHO WASN'T THERE* (JOEL AND ETHAN COEN, 2001)

The note of longing that creeps into the voice
of the woman who cuts my hair when she says
"Oh, it was *amazing*"—she is speaking of the time

she was twenty-one and went for a weeklong cruise
around the Virgin Islands on a friend's sailboat—
is so heartfelt, so hushed,

so purely human that it makes me wonder
what parts of the story she is leaving out,
what she isn't saying, which suspends itself,

as the unsaid always does, like a shadow or aura
over the words she has allowed herself to say.
Meanwhile her scissors sing the *snip snip snip*

of revision, and small seed-packets of my hair
are drifting to the floor as if through humid forest
air. As always I have let it grow too long

and have come in looking like a middle-aged professor
of philosophy who is trying to look a little
like Roger Daltrey, or, if he's lucky, Robert Plant;

a gesture, perhaps, toward the life I get to live
in the alternative plotline, the deleted scenes
hidden in my life's Special Edition DVD.

■

Desire is always a hazardous thing
to reveal. That bold, slightly unfed look
you direct without intending to toward a stranger

you suddenly want—does she remind you of your mother,
or your first girlfriend, or does she represent
the possibility of an alternate life,

one very much like this one in all the ways that matter,
but deeper, more pure?—either risks breaking apart
the social fabric, or else, if only we could see it,

is the very glue that binds the social fabric
together. *Thread* being, perhaps, in this context,
a slightly more fitting metaphor than *glue*.

■

Never having been to the Virgin Islands,
having been twenty-one, having experienced
unfulfilled longing, never having been a woman,

I am able partly, but only partly
to imagine what she is feeling, as she
herself, perhaps, is forced in large part to imagine

the things her younger self used to feel—
memory being, according to its very nature,
fragmented and incomplete, edited

very much in the way that film is put together:
jump cuts, dissolves, montages, eyeline matching,
flashbacks and flash-forwards, all to tell the story.

Hence the tearstained and wistful delicious twin pleasures
of imagining and remembering, the flickering beam
of light emanating from somewhere behind you

and the shadows it gives life to, the murmur of the huddled
breathing bodies all around you, the encompassing dark
that inhales and embraces, that exhales and resolves.

MY BOOK

I bought a copy, but it wasn't mine.
I stole a copy. Still it felt somehow
as if it did not yet belong to me.
As if I did not yet belong to it.
So I sat down to write it. As the sun
fingered the moon's pale skin and shed its own,
my fingers made my pen push glossy ink
across the page. Out in the fields, the cows
sang ancient songs of mourning and of mating,
while in the boxes that contained the humans,
the humans sat before their boxes. Still
I wrote, and though I did not comprehend
even an insubstantial fragment of
what that blood-thick black ink was saying, what
I knew was that when it was done, I'd have
grown older, the grimy globe would have grown older,
and on my shelf would sit my book, a shrunken
governor of an antique Chinese province,
surveying all that came within his purview,
including me, and passing judgment on it.

GOING VIRAL

> My face is my mask.
> —GUMP WORSLEY

Nothing is weirder than the human face.
Fortunately, we are not permitted
to see it very often.

The masks
and the lighting
take care of that.

■

Pray for me, she said,
and then
Wait,
I meant to say
pay for me.

■

I have had my way with your image
so many times—when you stand
at the edge
of the cliff
and sway—
can you really say
my despair
is no part of what you feel?

■

You can't give away the virtues
these days, and I have none
to offer anyway.

Only these silent hands,
their heavy weakness,
their inscrutable signs.

■

But is it the emptiness
of the left hand that you want,
or the emptiness
of the right?

One of them holds the pick.
One of them presses down
on the strings. And one of them
stretches
without ever daring to touch
to stroke to caress
the beloved's neck.

■

Four thousand years ago
we all inhabited
the same tiny bulletproof egg.

■

Were you two close?
someone asked,
and I replied *yes,*
I was too close.

BONE

Church-white, hard, and hollow.
The shaft of an arrow.
A conductor's baton,
or the mast of a schooner
abandoned but on
its course still. Who knew
how it came to me,
came to be among
my relics,
part of my retinue?

Part of me thought
it was part of me,
a leftover piece
from my first assembly.
I wanted to swallow it,
let it inside,
where it would divine
its place and leave me
flawless, voidless,
unfallen, un-hollow,
and happily unified:
human frame and meat,
a body finally at peace,
at last rendered complete.

Instead I carried it
everywhere,
sliding my thumb
along the smooth length

of the little spear,
trying to touch,
with my mind, the mind
of the dead and dismantled
beast that had once
called itself its home.
But I could not, for
I could not even
put a name on its kind:

Jackrabbit? Coyote?
Mountain lion?
Not snake, not turtle,
not fish. If a bird,
large, a predator,
something that cast
a broad shadow, something
majestic and fierce.
With the moon flat and vast
in my window, I'd lie
on my bed, my head
rampant and fertile
with beauty.

On the school grounds
I had to conceal
my small totem.
Authorities would
see only a weapon.
At recess I stuck it
in a small pile
of ground,
making a sundial,
a compass.
It pointed in every direction.
It was confusing,
but it was okay.

At that age,
every direction
was good.
All of them meant
away.

POSSESSION

Is there anything anywhere in this world
that is free from possession, that is not owned
by anyone? If there is, I want it.

I have cleared a space for it
in the corner of my bedroom. I will put it
there, and let everyone know that I have it,

and envy will fill them as poured tea fills
a cup. *Why did I not think to make
it mine?* they will ask themselves, and they

will receive no answer. So they will come
to admire it, bringing their envy with them
like an offering. And it will feel as if there

is light inside me, I will feel the way
the gods feel, for the envy of others makes us
divine. I just need to figure out what

this thing is and where I might find it. The things
I have found thus far are already labeled
and claimed. Tell me, where is the unattached thing?

DEATH BY LANDSCAPE

And what if the matter of your body
were suddenly to remember all
that it has in common with the atoms
that compose these oaks and alders,
that the music of meteors tumbling from their fixed
positions is also the music of your lungs
as they expand and pause
and hold still like a thing that has passed, like a thing
that has fallen into shadow,
and then, like a fist in anger, tighten?

And the music of the vast dust clouds, hurtling
outward from their unimaginable emptying
centers at speeds that themselves cannot
be imagined?

There is the fear of being swallowed by a landscape,
of stepping into a canoe
and knowing, as it gently tugs itself
out from under your foot, that you will not
return to that shore. Like waking in an unknown
bed and searching frantically through
gusts and waves of dimly remembered fragments
for *anything* solid: your weapon, your faith. . . .

And there is the urge to speak your name in empty places.
And there is the sadness of hands, of teeth.

SECOND WIND

The white of the ocean's foam-froth is said
to contain all colors, while the sea's green-blue depths
are composed of the colors our ancestors could
not bear. Or could not bear to let go:
the story varies with the source.
And the shadow that lies on the sea is cast

by no flying or orbiting thing, but by
the ocean floor where it blocks the light
from the sun at the heart of the earth. These things,
however they might terrify, are nonetheless
true. I will hold you through the shivers
and terrors. I will kiss the unholy curve
of your neck. I will try to take your mind

off the shadow. It is the shape of a tree.
There is the brusque sound of the branches as they
caress the wind. Its black silhouette
against the calamitous sunset. The darkness
that lives at its core. What the leaves know
and do not tell the roots. And what the roots know.

THE BLACK-CAPPED CHICKADEES OF
MARTHA'S VINEYARD

1

What are birds, what can they be if not
objectified thoughts? That scarlet tanager
an idea about beauty, that American redstart
the memory of a hotel on the Oregon
coast, where you stayed for three days, while the things
you thought you'd understood fell to pieces around you . . .

2

The black-capped chickadee is native to most
of North America, and everywhere its song
is the same. Everywhere, that is, except
on Martha's Vineyard. The black-capped chickadees
of Martha's Vineyard sing the standard
black-capped chickadee song: *hey sweetie,*
hey sweetie—but they sing, as well, a pair
of variations: *sweetie hey, sweetie hey,*
and *soweetie-sweetie, soweetie-sweetie.*
Recordings exist and can be consulted.
As for explanations, the human
researchers who study these things
assure us that they are forthcoming.

3

First you learn to cause pain, then the task is to learn
to live with having caused pain. There are places

where the mind is permitted to wander unleashed,
and you learn, over time, where the gates are, who keeps them,
under what conditions you will be allowed
to pass unobstructed. You learn the dialects
of rivers, which gestures in which territories
are taken as insults. Knowledge is stored
in the brain in folds of tissue, as is
the memory of your first lover's face,
the melody line of "Someone to Watch
Over Me," and your opinion as to which
of the dozen or so versions of that song
you have heard is the sweetest, the most beautiful,
the most haunting. Though of course your opinion
is subject to change, to a minor rearrangement
of the tissues, one that might be caused
by a shower of petals, an oddly placed word
in an argument with a friend, or happening
to hear that song on the radio
while driving while cruising the stations or in
a quiet, slightly musty Parisian café
that you ducked into only to try to escape from
the spatter of rain that came out of the sky
with no warning, from nowhere at all. *Sweetie, hey.*

4

The nightingale, Pliny writes, is "the only
bird the notes of which are modulated
according to the strict principles
of musical science." Each one, he goes on
to tell us, has its own repertoire
of songs, deployed in the musical battles
they conduct against one another. "The vanquished one
frequently perishes in the contest,
and would rather yield its life than its song."

The part of me that would like to believe this
has taken to walking the creekside trails
late in the evening, when the darkening sky
turns shade after deepening shade of blue,
hoping to meet, by chance, if chance
is the word, the twilit part of you
that would also like to believe this, which
is also the part, if I'm not mistaken,
that wishes it could love something, anything,
with the same unembarrassed rush of passion
the dying nightingale feels for its song.
The part of you that stood in the open
doorway in a white dress and said
You can talk about love all you like, you're a poet.
You'd rather sing about it than live through it.

5

What I know is this: when you are done learning
how to cause pain, which you never are,
you learn how not to, which you never do.

And what I know is this: early this morning,
in the branches of my neighbor's oleander,
I saw a spot of flame, a spark-red
northern cardinal, out of place
and out of season. Surely, my love,
that has to count for something.

III   ON BLINDNESS

True, in the blind years I certainly experienced beauty—in music, in bird songs, in the wind, in holding lovely shapes and forms. Now, however, to the sound of the wind is added the movement of tall grasses and white clouds; to the music the instrument; to the birdsong, the bird.

—ROBERT HINE, *SECOND SIGHT*

ON BLINDNESS

Saint Francis of Assisi, so the legend goes,
wept floods of tears so vast his eyes abandoned sight.

Was it excess of salt, or could so lachrymose
a man simply not bear, or dare admit, the light?

No one can say, for none today can diagnose,
the DNA having so many years ago

been mis-assigned, to linger next to or behind—
one must imagine this—a flabby cardboard box,

unlabeled and untouched. Inside, as like as not,
the rape kit that establishes beyond a doubt

that Leda's swan was Zeus, not some anonymous
and badly over-sauced, over-aggressive goose.

The fate of Oedipus is somewhat more complex:
his blinding was intentional, the consequence

of his eyes' having seen, to pinch a famous bit
from one-hit-wonder Charlene's one and only hit,

some things a human ain't supposed to see. And when
I think about the way John Milton's light was spent

I realize that to see is also to be blind
to what the seen conceals, the world that lurks behind

the well-lit screen on which the scene we see is seen.
They also serve who stand and wonder what this means.

THE APPLES

What gods have they fed, or failed to,
while I lingered on the wavering grass
watching men clutching dark gray briefcases
and sporting half-wilted beards enter and leave
the Museum of Absurdities, the harsh,
cinereal light playing on their shoulders,
sprinkled like salt in their black, fulsome hair?
What would a bowl of them be worth
that I might present to you, their glossy,
crepuscular skins glowing slightly, as if
they were making a promise, or, if not that,
as if they were half-remembering some promise
they had failed to keep? The night you and I
slowly climbed the steep stairs from the beach to the bluffs,
I thought I was on the verge of possessing
all I'd been wanting. Now three months
have passed, and somehow we still have yet
to reach the top.

The crisp, almost corky texture that meets
your teeth and tongue, the first bite's
violation of the orb's integrity,
its divine perfection—you want to draw
a moral out of it, a lesson,
but the apple has only itself to offer,
which is more than enough, or would be, if only
our hearts weren't made mostly of ash.
What gods have we entertained, or failed to,
in our relentless pursuit of solace,
of truth, of the soft parts of each other's bodies,

as we take the torch in our hands and pass it
into the hands of the next runner, not
noticing, or pretending not to notice,
that the flame was extinguished some decades ago,
if in fact it ever burned at all?

CHARLIE BROWN

When the little tree falters and droops pathetically
under the weight of that innocent-looking
but fatal ornament, and Charlie Brown wails
I've killed it, everything I touch gets ruined,
I *feel* for the guy: I know the sad prison
his heart's doing time in. I know how it feels
to be King Midas's evil twin,
Destructo-Man careening through the world,
smashing houses, reducing highways to rubble,
leveling whole cities with my evil-eye laser beams
and mega-grenades. If only I could hold
a cute little bunny without crushing the breath
out of it with my unrestrained strength, if only
I could embrace a woman without inspiring
in her the sudden desire to get
a restraining order or move to Cleveland.
I wish I could have a drink with Charlie
Brown—he must be old enough now,
he probably goes by Charles, or Chuck—
and tell him it gets better, Chuck, or, really,
it doesn't, but you learn to live with it,
and you learn that what you destroy comes back
to you, not always, but sometimes, refreshed
and reassembled, almost as good
as new, and sometimes—*sometimes*—bearing
the willingness to forgive. And he'd take
a long, mad gulp of his vodka gimlet,
stare off into a world that only
he is heartbroken and tipsy enough
to see—some planar Midwestern town

with repeating trees and ink-black night skies—
and, forgetting that I was there, he'd shake
that globe of a head and sigh and mutter
You know, the truth is that Linus was right.
It really wasn't such a bad little tree.

SOME MEN

A man wakes up
in a monastery
on a mountaintop
in Tibet,
having given all
his possessions away,
and cries out, "Dammit,
I'm still me!"
A man walks into
a martini bar
carrying a chainsaw
and we all wait
to see what will happen.
A priest, a rabbi,
and a Buddhist plumber
live in different neighborhoods
and never meet.
A man says,
"Take my wife, please,
to the emergency room.
She is bleeding badly."
Several men are running
as fast as they can
through the open door
of a martini bar.
Something is happening
inside. A man
wakes up in America,
filled with joy
to live in this land

of opportunity, where anyone,
regardless of race
or class, can grow up
and shoot the President.
A man puts a cat
in a box, connects
the box to a tube
that contains a toxic
substance, connects
the tube's lid to
a mechanical arm
that is, in turn,
hooked up to a computer
that monitors an isotope
that may or may not
decay in the next
twelve seconds. The cat's name
is Simon. The whole time
the man is thinking to
himself that for
at least ten years
he has felt—not dead,
exactly, but not quite
entirely alive.

THE PROSELYTIZERS

The proselytizers had a God they liked a lot and wanted people to hear about. But nearly everyone they tried to talk to already had their own God. So they started carrying two cases with them: a large one and a somewhat smaller one. They would set the large case, which looked like it contained some sort of machine, in the corner, where it would sit like a well-trained dog. From the smaller case they would take a pouch of dirt: dust, cigarette butts, coffee grounds. "Would you like to see a demonstration?" they would ask those who had been kind enough to open their doors to them. Then they would dump the dirt on the floor, in a little ugly pile. They would grind the dirt into the carpet with their heels until it looked like it was there for good. "There," they would say. "Now what do you think your God is going to do about that?"

UNIVERSAL

Bang, zoom, to the moon
the universe hisses
each time you resume
consciousness
in your dumb luck
dumbstruck room.
Bad news, but it could
be worse:
its cousin,
an even more mischievous
universe,
likes to crouch behind
a juniper bush
and jump out, screaming,
a windmilling ambush,
wearing a Richard
Nixon mask,
each time our protagonist
wanders past.

Why this universe,
or that one? Why
these weird colors? Why
the contingency
of not speaking French,
of having hands,
of being named *Leroy*,
Philip, or *Hans*,
of liking cold cuts,
hot jazz, cold climates,

hot chocolate, cold fusion,
hot sex, hot showers,
of being turned on
by pineapple-shaped breasts,
by an unexpected
bouquet of flowers,
by the sound of rain
in the trees, by the way
some women pronounce
the word *Belize*?

Why any
universe at all?
The jury is still out,
although every
punk and professor
has his pet theory.
"Why is there something
rather than nothing?"
Sidney Morgenbesser
was asked to explain.
He is said to have said,
in response, "Even if
there was nothing,
you'd still complain."

PHOTOGRAPH

That photo of you at twenty:
why could you never see before how sad you were?
She is peering into the camera
as if it were a telescope, and she could see
you through it, miles and years away,
a tiny figure whispering *Come on through, come on through,*
it hurts here, too, but we can start again together.

POLAROID MODEL 1000 ONESTEP, CIRCA 1978

It might have been passed away at a yard
or garage sale, to other hands who hoped
to preserve, with it, from time and the gathering,
unrepentant dark, some image worth
saving. More likely it got shipped out
in one of the many cartons of detritus
our collapsing lives ejected, to end up
flattened and crushed in some landfill or other,
its memories vacated and extinguished
like dreams that seem, during the first few
moments of wakefulness, to be vivid
enough to last, but which then
dissipate like soap bubbles into the air.

It never took very good pictures anyway:
the light flat, the colors garish and maudlin.
If it mattered, it mattered only because
it was our constant companion, there for
every family gathering and backyard
barbecue, a perpetual witness
to graduations and prom nights, a staunch
observer of fabrics and outfits long and,
in most cases, better forgotten (so many
awful oranges and browns!)
Little unassuming recorder and friend
of pets who have long since fetched their last,
our family talisman, carried
on every vacation, it left us a permanent

record of everything but its own
existence and presence. It could not acknowledge
itself. And it didn't occur to any
of us, not once, to hold it up to a mirror.

ARS POETICA

I'm not in very much pain these days
is a terrible way to start a poem
because the poet's pain is what puts the asses
in the seats, it's the half-nude neon
lady on the sign outside
the strip club, it's the guy with the big
yellow twirling arrow outside the furniture
store, and without the poet's pain,
what do you have? Some pretty words
about barn swallows and oleanders,
some standard verses re: lovely lakes
and the midnight water laps softly, peace
sneaking up behind you on tender cat pads,
etc., etc. . . . . The poet's pain
is his bread and butter, his keys to the kingdom,
his ace in the hole. It's what you take away
from him when it's the last act and you really
want to grind his pathetic rhyme-spitting face
in the gravel. It's what the world has gifted
him, and damn him if he won't carry it
out of the kitchen on a big
precariously balanced silver platter, furiously
steaming. No one needs, or wants, or should even
be asked to tolerate a happy poet.
I'm feeling fine, the therapy is going well
are words that should never appear
in a poem. The game cannot be won
and will be called on account of darkness.
Our rhymes whack away at the world like hatchets
thrown into a dead wet stump. No wonder

so many people keep dying, what
with all the elegies we keep writing.
Let's take a break, some suggest. Yes,
but poetry makes nothing happen, and so
can hardly be blamed for this. Would
that this were true. Would that people would stop
beginning sentences that aren't questions
with the word *would*. You might as well just
wear a billboard around your neck that says
I'm a poet, come fondle my sensitive soul,
lick my barbaric yawp, for I know
what the songs have promised me. Actually,
I never found out what the songs had intended
to promise me. I only know
that I never received it. Was someone supposed
to take me aside at some point and whisper it
into my ear? Or write it on
the underside of a cup of coffee
that got served to me somewhere? Is there still
a chance that this might happen?
Tell the gods, tell the singers of songs,
tell the ghosts that I'm ready.

THE NEW JOYS

We are free now to do whatever we like,
and the new joys, the unprecedented ecstasies,
are laid out before us like a platoon
of dead birds on a long wooden table, cooked
to perfection, birds of every size and species,
not just the usual turkeys and hens
but blue jays, egrets, ravens, storks, pelicans,
slow-roasted penguins stuffed with wild spinach
and garnished with blue cheese, pan-fried oriole
served on a bed of polenta beside
sliver-spears of succulent sweet potato,
and even, right there at the center of things,
a majestic clay-baked cassowary. We savor
it all, first with our starved human eyes
as we balance goblets of wine and make small
polite trite conversation, before at last
we are permitted to shed our pretentions
of civilization and snatch the shardlike
utensils and charge like happy barbarians
into this battlefield, into this feast
of delicate birdsflesh. We are allowed
to do this only because we will one day
be feasted upon, we eat and we will be
eaten, we consume and one day we will be
consumed, just as we forget and will one day
be forgotten. And tonight after we
have feasted we'll leave the servants to deal with
the plates and I will carry you back
to my room and take off your dress, I will lift it
over your head like a man removing

the feathers from the skin of a duck
he has just shot out of the sky, and I
will cradle you in my arms, a small
denuded soft shivering thing,
and you'll say to me *can I tell you about it
again*, and I will say *yes,* and your chastened
lips will whisper, not for the last time,
just one more time, this will be the last time.

IV WHEN YOU LIFT THE AVOCADO TO YOUR MOUTH

No, no, no, no! Come, let's away to prison.
We two alone will sing like birds i' the cage.
—SHAKESPEARE, *KING LEAR*, ACT 5, SCENE 3

TAMARA

Years from now he'll remember the nights he spent
trying to unlock a lock of her hair
and how, when she kissed him, he felt like a poem
being translated from one language into another.

THE TASK

A man is carrying a card with him everywhere he goes. It is a five-by-eight index card that drifted to the floor a few days ago when he opened a library copy of Italo Calvino's *Invisible Cities*. The handwriting on the card is familiar and he wonders whether it is his. It is not the way he writes now but it might be that he wrote like this at some point in his life. Perhaps he was more extravagant with his gestures back then, perhaps he has since learned not to draw so much attention to himself. But it makes no sense, he thought at first, because he has never read this book before. But when he started reading it he realized that in fact he had read it, years ago; it was not, as he had been thinking, one of those books he had been pretending to have read when he hadn't really, but rather a book that he had read and that he only thought he was pretending to have read.

But the copy that he had read could not have been this particular copy, for that must have been years before he moved to this city. No, it was a different copy, one that he had owned, a paperback purchased from Second Story Books in Washington, DC. He could picture that particular copy, its particular coffee stains, specific as fingerprints. Except that he realizes, a day or two later, that that book was not in fact a copy of *Invisible Cities*. It was a copy of *Cosmicomics*, also by Italo Calvino. That copy, moreover, had never belonged to him; it had been the possession of a friend, from whom he had borrowed it and to whom he had returned it shortly before, for reasons he cannot now remember, the friendship dissolved. And when he pauses to count the years since leaving Washington he realizes that he has been living here much longer than he had at first thought. So even if it has been several years since he read the book—and he is not, at this point, entirely sure of this—this does not prove that he had to have read it somewhere else.

Still, the handwriting is different, and the ink—would he have chosen that shade of blue? Though maybe he had simply borrowed someone's pen.

What bothers him most, though, is the content of what is written on the card, not only because it feels like something he might once have thought but would certainly not think now, but because of the urgency with which the note seems to have been written, the way it seems to be calling on him to perform a task he could not possibly now fulfill, the way that, although it is now a decade and a half too late, it will not seem to release him from the necessity of performing an action that he cannot be certain was ever his to perform.

MORE BROKEN THAN YOURS

1

You might rule this town
with your proud tin crown
but my heart is more broken than yours.

2

You might fashion a spliff-scented web every night,
but I toss all my coins off the pier each day.

3

Keep in mind, you might have made love to all
the magicians in town, but I am the one
who scattered their prize nightingales in the suburbs'
relentless interstices, even as deployments
of renegade hummingbirds bearded my throat.

4

My throat, which they may have mistaken for
a version of their own, bedecked
as it was by a seething multitude of miniature
spice-scented ruby-tinted suck-buzzards.

5

I imagine you might well have wrapped them in dough
and baked them to a light crisp. You might well

have popped the delicious small fledglings into
your mouth, one by one, as you blithely perused
the Real Estate section of the *L.A. Times.*

6

And lest you forget, or pretend to forget,
let me remind you that I am the one
who retrieved the fragrances of the stars
from the far barbarian camps, and unfolded
a chair alongside the fishmonger's tent
where I offered to daub those recovered scents
behind the delicate, overlooked ears
of our high society ladies.

7

Ladies who would step forward one
by one, offering their denuded necks
as if it were an axe I held in my hands.

FIREWORKS

First we tamed heat, and we called it fire.
Then we tamed light, and we called it the movies.
Then came the sky, such an obvious idea
we were kicking our unhelpful hands for hours,
and birds to puff up the little scars in it.
Fortune-tellers arrived the next day,
there was much spirit traffic in the streets,
and I decided I wanted to call you up
but we hadn't taught telephones how to ring yet.
People used to play with every part of
the pig back then, which is how you know
that we are in serious decline. Why not
declare war on those who think otherwise?
Egalitarianism may be in a soft
death spiral, but scientists tell us new forms
of thought will continue evolving in all sorts
of corners and crevices your average human
couldn't hope to finesse a finger into,
which might be a source of hope in dark times
and is, at any rate, something fine
to chat about idly at cocktail parties.
Tonight there will be fireworks, thousands of miles
from any human observer and on
the sub-molecular level. I'm going
to get a bottle of wine anyway,
and a lightweight folding picnic table.
I'm hoping that you'll come too.

LAMENT

No more swamp existence for you, with all
its pleasures, all that rooting around
in forgotten quarters for forgotten nickels.
No more meretricious jazz piano
eliding your way between gross destinations,
unreviewed memoirs by former conundrums,
videos of venal comebacking musicians
going viral on the spiral screen. No more
slowly starving cathedrals into being,
no more convalescing by feel, no more
nosing out the neglected harmonica part
that was meant to fluff out the flourish but got
buried so deep in the mix you could get
the bends coming up from that. No more
lonesome nights on the couch of the cute girl who
will never think of you as anything but
"that sad guy that sleeps on my couch sometimes."
No more paid lunch hours reciting quasi-
pornography in limbic pentameter, no more
coughing up eloquently Venn-diagrammed
faux-Whitmanesque vibes. No more driving everyone
nuts insisting that the less frequently
listened-to B-side is where the genius really lies.
No more perturbing the air with your smooth
but inscrutable pantomime gestures. No more
bop bop bopping along the *Via
Negativa* while grasping the dangling string
of a helium balloon bouquet with all
thy might, as if it somehow really mattered,
as if, if you could only hold on. . . .

No more lamenting the precipitous decline
of the panic industry, the sudden disappearance
of the Flightless Dough, the unforeseen renaissance
of the infidels with their zinfandels. No more
making goddamn sure that your goddamn verbs
agree with your goddamn nouns, no more
assaulting strangers with spray cheese in
the street to protest your parents' politics.
No more wet dreams, no more dry ice, no more
dry heaves, no more wetware, no more sad sacks,
the anti-world has given you notice,
there's no more *going* going, no more *coming* coming back.

THE FOURTEEN-HOUR ORGASM

After years of study and discipline he finally achieved his life's goal: the fourteen-hour orgasm. It happened one Tuesday morning, a gray day that threatened rain. After thirty seconds he knew this was it, and he felt ecstatic. After five minutes he got his first inkling of how exhausting it might become. Sometime early in the second hour his partner gathered her things and left for her job, leaving him alone in the house. He managed to drag himself to an armchair and sat facing the fireplace, waiting for it to be over. All day long people came to the door: proselytizers, Girl Scouts with cookies. They rang the doorbell, waited, rang again, and left. Meanwhile, he sat inside, an unhappy and increasingly desperate man, riding the wave of the greatest pleasure a human being had ever experienced.

NOT ENOUGH

There isn't enough
blue for the sky
and for the mountain jay.
There isn't enough
blue for my eyes and
for *Crows over a Wheatfield.*
There isn't enough
black for my pain
and for the ink it will
take to write
the letter that I am
writing to you
in which I describe,
in detail, my pain.
There isn't enough
black for 3 AM
and for the hole
in my eye that we call
the pupil, because
calling it the pupil
can help us forget
that it's a hole,
because holes in the body
make us nervous.
There isn't enough
green for the ripe
avocado I want to
pulverize into
guacamole
and for the envy

I feel when a friend
writes a good poem
or says something clever
that makes some girl's
eyes light up like she's
a pinball machine
and the bastard just
won a bonus round.
There isn't enough
silence for the empty
rooms where the old men
and women wait for hours
for news that can't be
anything but bad,
and to keep my words
from mashing
like awkward dancers
into each other.
There isn't enough
black for the hands
of the clock and for the
numbers on the dial.
There isn't enough
fear for my fear
of small confined spaces
and for my fear
that brute absurdity
is the foundation
on which the universe
is built, with nothing
rational beneath.
There isn't enough
forgetting to forget
all the wars we have fought—
you have to choose two
or three, and then just
resign yourself

to remembering the rest.
There isn't enough
red for the blood
that nourished the fields
of all those battles
and for the strawberries
and for the cherries
and for the cardboard
boxes of chocolates
that all the world's lovers
want from and for
each other as marks of
delight and desire
on Valentine's Day.
There isn't enough
night sky for the humans
to fall safely into
when at long last
the earth, as we all know
it will, fails us.
There isn't enough
solace for a single
human being,
let alone seven billion.
There isn't enough
silence for the silence
that swells against
my heart's inner face
when I think about
the silent space
the helpless creatures
whose fate it is to
grow into us
are born out of
and the spacious silence
the helpless creatures
it is our fate to

grow into will,
when night comes, be,
with the promise of no
parole and the promise
of no reprieve,
with the promise of no
announcement and
the promise of no
apology, thrust,
headlong and abrupt
and with a divine
brutality,
back into.

POEM FOR THE ABANDONED TITAN MISSILE SILOS JUST NORTH OF CHICO, CALIFORNIA

for Wilhelmina Taggart

The
perfection
of a species
is extinction.

We
all vanish
from the stage
sooner or later.

Some
of us just leave a
slightly
deeper crater.

AUTUMN DAY

after Rilke

Lord: it is time. The summer was so vast.
Now let your shadows darken the sundials,
while to the grassy field your winds are cast.

Send to the final fruits the order: *ripen.*
Grant them just two more balmy southern days,
and urge them to perfection. In this way
the heavy wine at last is forced to sweeten.

He that has made no home will have no home.
He that has found no friend will have no friend.
He'll waken, read, write letters that find no end,
walk out into the tree-lined streets, and roam
where the restless leaves wheel in the bitter wind.

THE SMALL RAIN

I have decided that today's small rain—
that drowsy sizzle in the frowzy trees,
which should begin, if I'm not wrong, at five past three—
will be dedicated to you

And I hope you'll take that yellow scrunchie from your hair
and walk out from your house into that downy shower
wearing that disheveled lemon sundress I've been aching
to see you wear

and just stand there

thinking of me as you do

WHEN YOU LIFT THE AVOCADO TO YOUR MOUTH

What matters is that when you lift the avocado to your mouth
you bend all your senses toward it, yet
allow a sliver of its flavor to escape
your lips—not into the muffled ether
of radio static that deadens the air
around us, but into the nearly real lips
of those who have gone before us, the pale
blue shadow-forms of the ancestors
who no longer have bodies to touch or to taste with,
to sing or to fuck with, but who still recall
what it is to touch or taste or sing or fuck
and who long for it and, in their longing, attach
themselves to the living, incarnated ones,
in the hope of feeling, once more, by a process
that must be mostly imagination, some spark
of sensation, the thinnest, outermost layer
of the experience of hearing the ocean,
of watching the moon rise over a city,
of kissing a woman, of stroking the fur
of a cat as it stretches to meet your palm,
of holding a pen, of smelling the pine-scented
breezes at dusk, of gazing deep into
a fire, a river, the eyes of a lover,
of tasting a teardrop, of tasting avocado.

V   VERTIGO

The poets use the birds merely as symbols of the unattainable . . .

—WALTER GARSTANG, *SONGS OF THE BIRDS*

VERTIGO

for Amber

We are each other's memories, when
our memories fail us. Like trying to re-
construct a movie seen long ago,

a movie that can't now be seen.
Like trying to reconstruct a time,
long ago, when the movie could not be seen

(since now everything is available, *on
demand,* and what cannot be had
on demand does not exist). A line

of dialogue. The slant of a face.
Like trying to solve a mystery,
a story that makes no sense, the return

of someone from the place from which
return is not allowed. Like trying
to reconstruct a person whom

you loved, who fell into the void.
Like following someone else's wife
around a city that is no more,

a "private eye"—we are each other's
eyes—trying to find out what
is possessing her, is possessing you.

■

I never tried to tell you
about the trio
of flawless cerulean eggs—

this is from years ago—
I found near the top
of a tree I had climbed, and how

I imagined
that the half-formed bird-to-be
encased in each like a precious stone

in its setting was dreaming
of the world
it had yet to be torn into;

I could picture, or so I thought,
the three embryonic dreams
hovering over the nest—

they looked, to my inner eye,
like pale smudgy shadows,
or wan ectoplasmic clouds—

and the spectral cord
that tethered
each one to its delicate shell.

■

When he sees her, Judy, in the street,
he knows. His body knows. She is dead,
officially, but this is the body,

his body knows, that he undressed
after he pulled her from the bay
she had fallen into (though the director

coyly elided the scene of her
unwrapping—we always see less than
we think in Hitchcock's films, which is how,

in the end, we see more). The body that stood
beside him counting the rings of the great
sequoia, that time-slice of history;

the body that disappeared without
explanation from the hotel to which
he had trailed her, that sat, enraptured, before

the portrait of Carlotta. *The things
that spell San Francisco to me are
disappearing fast.* And when they return,

it is for one purpose only:
so that they can disappear again,
and more decisively than before.

■

Nor did I ever try
to tell you about
the bleached sliver of bone

that I used to carry around
in my backpack,
a ghostly compass needle

that longed, when it rained, for water.
I did not know
what kind of creature

it had come from or
what part of the body
of that unknown animal

it had at one time
inhabited. But somehow,
having it felt lucky—

one of those silly
superstitions
collected and deployed to try

to keep the vast, inscrutable,
unmanageable world
at bay.

■

What if a color—let's say blue—
simply disappeared? From the sky,
the ocean, from films, from magazines,

and when you tried to bring it up
no one else claimed to remember it.
The sky has always looked like that,

they'd say. How long would it be before
you believed them? And how long would it be
that you would continue to dream in blue?

■

"The partial and
complete extinction
of many races and sub-races

of man are historically
known events.
Humboldt saw in South America

a parrot which was
the sole living creature
that could speak the language of

a lost tribe." (Darwin,
The Descent of Man,
and Selection in Relation to Sex)

■

This is how men use
her, how they make her
into someone else. Or is it

possible that
she enjoys this, that
she likes being Madeleine, is it even

possible that
Madeleine might be—
whatever, precisely, this might be taken

to mean—the *real* her?
And Scottie, in forcing
her to transform, actually is

fulfilling her deepest
desire, as well as his,
resurrecting his lost love?

Not part of a plot,
except insofar
as the world itself is a plot.

The title of
the original novel,
D'entre les morts, is typically

translated as
From among the Dead,
but it can also be rendered as

From between the Deaths,
which is better, perhaps,
insofar as this version gestures toward

the numinous
and precarious void
over which our lives are suspended, and

reminds us that every
life exists
"between the deaths"—a spark, a moment

of brightness strung tight
like a thread, an interregnum
between eternities,

during each of which
the projector sits inert,
and the screen is blank.

■

Nor did I ever
get to tell you
of the awful experiments

in which pressure sensors
are surgically implanted
into the skulls of songbirds,

or the nerves that connect
the syrinx to the brain
are snipped, in order to determine

which severings leave them
able to sing,
and which ones leave them silent.

So much madness in
the pursuit of beauty,
in pursuit of the understanding of beauty.

■

It's not just his fear of heights,
his terror of falling,
that Gavin Elster must count on,

but also that Scottie,
not having fallen
to his death, will fall,

that he will fall
in love with Madeleine
at first sight. One glimpse and he takes

the case. And just so,
in the scene
at Ernie's, Madeleine's lovely face

must claim us too,
must seduce us, so that
we are rendered ready

when, in the next scene,
we see Scottie
already stalking her through the streets

of that charmed city. And
it does. We do.
And when she screams and falls

into the void,
and dies—
and part of Scottie falls and dies with her—

and when she screams
and falls, and dies,
a part of us falls, too.

∎

The attention to detail that is required
to re-create a film, a moment,
a human being, a restaurant

that doesn't exist anymore
is enormous:
the dialogue must be right,

the lighting, the dress, the hair.
And all that with only
one's memories to go on.

And then there is that indefinable
thing: the angle of the eye,
the way a certain word is said,

and what is being remembered,
what small wish
or regret or confession

is passing through
the mind like a scythe of wind
through a field of wheat—

but oh, the reward for getting it right,
the embrace that is the reward, such an
embrace as mere mortals can scarcely imagine . . .

■

We are each other's
privacies. We are
each other's solitudes.

We are the living
forms in which
beauty can be encountered and

pursued. And we are
made for looking,
made to be looked at, and made

to fall and to
remember and
to fall again. And we are made

for loving, and
for dying. We are
made to be unmade.

■

There is so much I
would like to tell you.
Instead, I carry and reread your letters,

your small handwriting
plaintive, increasingly
poignant in the gathering dark.

I used to say, *just enjoy*
the questions, you write
in one. *But now, more and more,*

it seems to me
that I would like
some answers after all. And, in

the last, *I feel*
like a swimmer, who has
ventured too far out, and who

is drowning in language,
and my own cries
for help are smothering me.

VI   CONCLUDING UNSCIENTIFIC POSTSCRIPT

The birds are the opposite of Time.
—OLIVIER MESSIAEN, PROGRAM NOTES FOR *QUARTET FOR THE END OF TIME*

[MAYBE I JUST NEED TIME TO GRIEVE]

maybe I just need time to grieve
the things we come to, the things we leave,

the sundew's seed, the snake's shed skin,
the dim-lit bar I found you in,

the winter mirror you cloud with your breath,
our city's slow death,

the songs your mother used to sing
before you were you, she was she, before anything

was anything

Notes and Acknowledgments

Much of the language of the poem "Syllabus of Errors" is drawn from the journals of Leonardo da Vinci, translated by Edward MacCurdy.

Several of the poems are informed by Don Stap's *Birdsong*, David Rothenberg's *Why Birds Sing: A Journey into the Heart of Birdsong*, and Walter Garstang's *Songs of the Birds*.

"Homer" was written in response to Byron Wolfe's photograph, *Backyard Baseball, About One Year Old*.

"Vertigo" is dedicated to Amber Harkins.

In an earlier version of "Universal" I got the Sidney Morgenbesser quotation wrong. I owe thanks to Howard Wettstein and Eric Schwitzgebel of the University of California, Riverside for pointing this out and helping me (and insisting that I) get it right. And for some other things, too.

The complete list of people who have been kind to me over the past few years would require a separately published volume, but a list of people who have in one way or another contributed to these poems, or who have helped me avoid or fix errors of one sort or another, would have to include Heather Altfeld, Amy Antongiovanni, David Baker, Aaron Belz, Michael Collier, Kevin Craft, Natalie Diaz, Matthew Dickman, Robin Ekiss, Becky Foust, Daisy Fried, John Gallaher, Forrest Gander, Linda Gregerson, Robert Hass, Brenda Hillman, Robert C. Jones, Joy Katz, John Koethe, Joey "Henry Fucking Kissinger" Mahoney, John "It's Fucking Tolerable" Mahoney, George Murray, Meryl Natchez, Sharon Olds, Carl Phillips, Doug Powell, Kevin Prufer, Dean Rader, Larry Rafferty, James Richardson, Don Share, Sheri Simons, Ed Skoog, Bruce Snider, Oscar Villalon, Byron Wolfe, Gary Young, and Matthew Zapruder. As with all such lists, there is no doubt that someone important has been omitted.

The author would also like to thank Philz Coffee in San Francisco and Berkeley for their coffee, and the Naked Lounge in Chico, California for their cappuccinos.

Poems in this book have or will have appeared in the following publications:

The Believer: "When You Lift the Avocado to Your Mouth"
Best Canadian Poetry in English 2015: "Some Men"
Birmingham Poetry Review: "Ars Poetica," "Syllabus of Errors"
Connotation Press: An Online Artifact: "The New Joys," "Not Enough"
Copper Nickel: "The Black-Capped Chickadees of Martha's Vineyard"
Exile: The Literary Quarterly: "More Broken than Yours," "Universal"
Laurel Review: "Going Viral"
Narrative Magazine: "On Birdsong"
New England Review: "The Apples," "Critique of Judgment"
New Poems: "Some Men"
The New Yorker: "My Book"
Okey-Panky: "Fireworks," "Lament," "Oriole"
Poetry: "Homer"
Poetry Northwest: "Bone," "Inventory," "Photograph," "Polaroid Model 1000 OneStep, Circa 1978"
Poets.org: "On the Origins of Things"
Rattle: "Cutting Room," "Tamara"
Tin House: "Past Imperfect"
The Walrus: "Charlie Brown"
Washington Square: "On Blindness"
Zyzzyva: "Death by Landscape," "Second Wind," "Vertigo"

Princeton Series of Contemporary Poets

An Alternative to Speech, David Lehman

And, Debora Greger

An Apology for Loving the Old Hymns, Jordan Smith

Armenian Papers: Poems 1954–1984, Harry Mathews

At Lake Scugog: Poems, Troy Jollimore

Before Recollection, Ann Lauterbach

Blessing, Christopher J. Corkery

Boleros, Jay Wright

Carnations: Poems, Anthony Carelli

The Double Witness: Poems, 1970–1976, Ben Belitt

A Drink at the Mirage, Michael J. Rosen

The Eternal City: Poems, Kathleen Graber

The Expectations of Light, Pattiann Rogers

An Explanation of America, Robert Pinsky

For Louis Pasteur, Edgar Bowers

A Glossary of Chickens: Poems, Gary J. Whitehead

Grace Period, Gary Miranda

Hybrids of Plants and of Ghosts, Jorie Graham

In the Absence of Horses, Vicki Hearne

The Late Wisconsin Spring, John Koethe

Listeners at the Breathing Place, Gary Miranda

Movable Islands: Poems, Debora Greger

The New World, Frederick Turner

Night Talk and Other Poems, Richard Pevear

The 1002nd Night, Debora Greger

Operation Memory, David Lehman

Pass It On, Rachel Hadas

Poems, Alvin Feinman

The Power to Change Geography, Diana O'Hehir

Reservations: Poems, James Richardson

Returning Your Call: Poems, Leonard Nathan

River Writing: An Eno Journal, James Applewhite

The Ruined Elegance: Poems, Fiona Sze-Lorrain

Sadness and Happiness: Poems, Robert Pinsky
Selected Poems, Jay Wright
Shores and Headlands, Emily Grosholz
Signs and Wonders: Poems, Carl Dennis
Syllabus of Errors: Poems, Troy Jollimore
The Tradition, Albert F. Moritz
The Two Yvonnes: Poems, Jessica Greenbaum
Visiting Rites, Phyllis Janowitz
Walking Four Ways in the Wind, John Allman
Wall to Wall Speaks, David Mus
A Wandering Island, Karl Kirchwey
The Way Down, John Burt
Whinny Moor Crossing, Judith Moffett
A Woman Under the Surface: Poems and Prose Poems, Alicia Ostriker
Yellow Stars and Ice, Susan Stewart